Annotation

Welcome to a fun and engaging journey designed for young learners! This book is packed with activities and lessons to help children build essential skills in language, communication, and social understanding while having a great time.

In Language and Communication, kids will explore recognizing letters from A to Z, counting numbers from 1-10 and beyond to 20, and identifying shapes like circles, squares, and triangles. They'll also grasp the concept of sizes, such as big/small and long/short, making learning both interactive and relatable.

Children will discover the magic of Seasons and Weather, from sunny days to rainy showers and snowy wonders. They'll also learn the importance of Basic Hygiene and Body Parts, gaining valuable knowledge on keeping clean and understanding their bodies.

Building strong relationships is a key focus, with activities on Recognizing Family Roles and exploring the dynamics of friendships and cooperation. Through these lessons, children will learn the importance of kindness, teamwork, and good manners like saying "please" and "thank you."

To sharpen problem-solving skills, the book includes Simple Mazes to complete and activities that encourage identifying differences and similarities. These exercises are designed to boost cognitive development and foster a sense of accomplishment.

Every picture in this book can and must be colored by the child, turning each page into a creative adventure. Additionally, 50% of the text is written in the form of poems, enhancing rhythm, engagement, and learning in a delightful way.

This book provides a holistic approach to early childhood education, blending creativity, knowledge, and practical skills. It's perfect for young minds eager to learn and explore. Dive into the pages, and watch as your child grows in confidence, curiosity, and joy!

This Book Belongs to:

_____

How to Use This Book

To make the most of this book, here are a few tips to prepare and engage your child in a fun and creative learning journey:

- **Gather Supplies:** Have color pencils or pens ready for coloring activities. These will add creativity and excitement to the learning experience.

- **Bring Extra Paper:** Keep some extra blank paper handy for additional drawings, notes, or practicing new skills.

- **Encourage Coloring:** Let your child color all the available pictures in the book as they progress through the activities. This not only sparks creativity but also reinforces the lessons learned.

Enjoy this interactive adventure together, combining learning and creativity to make education a joyful experience!

PART I

The Alphabet
Recognize letters (A-Z) and begin early word formation.

The Alphabet Adventure

A is for **Apple**, so juicy and red,
B is for **Ball**, you can bounce on your head.
C is for **Cat**, with a soft little purr,
D is for **Duck**, quack-quacking for sure.

E is for **Elephant**, so big and so strong,
F is for **Fish**, swimming all day long.
G is for **Giraffe**, with a neck oh so high,
H is for **Hat**, sitting up in the sky.

I is for **Igloo**, so chilly and cold,
J is for **Jelly**, so wobbly and bold.
K is for **Kite**, flying up with the breeze,
L is for **Lion**, the king of the trees.

M is for **Monkey**, swinging with glee,
N is for **Nest**, in the tall, leafy tree.
O is for **Orange**, sweet and round,
P is for **Penguin**, waddling around.

Q is for **Queen**, with a crown so grand,
R is for **Rainbow**, brightening the land.
S is for **Star**, shining at night,
T is for **Train**, chugging in flight.

U is for **Umbrella**, keeping you dry,
V is for **Violin**, playing notes so high.
W is for **Whale**, splashing in the sea,
X Is for **Xylophone**, making music with glee.

Y is for **Yoyo**, spinning up and down,
Z is for **Zebra**, with stripes all around.
Now you've learned the alphabet rhyme,
Sing it again—it's learning time!

A is Amazing!

A is for **Apple**, shiny and red,
Crunch it for breakfast, or just before bed.

A is for **Alligator**, swimming with might,
Snapping its jaws in the warm sunlight.

A is for **Airplane**, up in the sky,
Zooming and soaring, oh my, oh my!

A is for **Ant**, so tiny and small,
Carrying food, it's strong for its size after all.

A is for **Alphabet**, let's sing it today,
Learning is fun in every way!

So here's to the letter, so awesome, so bright,
A starts adventures, morning till night!

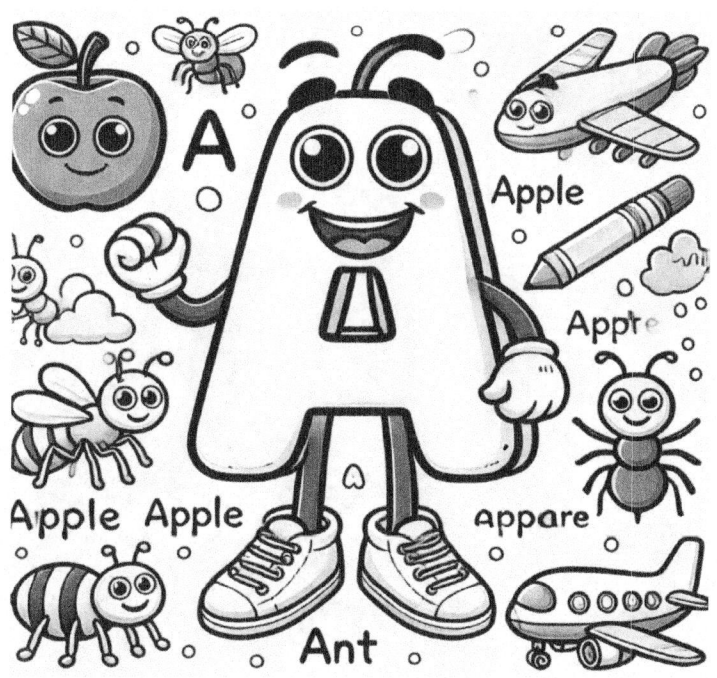

B is the Best!

B is for **Ball**, bouncing so high,
Throw it, catch it, give it a try!

B is for **Bee**, buzzing around,
Making sweet honey, a buzzing sound.

B is for **Boat**, floating on the lake,
Sailing so smoothly, leaving a wake.

B is for **Bear**, big and so bold,
Cuddly and soft, or wild in the cold.

B is for **Banana**, yummy and sweet,
Peel it and munch, a tasty treat!

B is so busy, with so much to do,
Let's learn together—me and you!

C is Cool!

C is for **Cat**, so furry and sweet,
Purring and napping by your feet.

C is for **Car**, zooming so fast,
Racing by, it's a total blast!

C is for **Cake**, a yummy delight,
With candles to blow on your birthday night.

C is for **Cow**, out in the field,
Giving us milk, what a great deal!

C is for **Cloud**, floating in the sky,
Soft and fluffy, way up high.

C is so cheerful, let's give it a cheer,
It's a letter we love, loud and clear!

D is Delightful!

D is for **Dog**, so loyal and true,
Wagging its tail and playing with you.

D is for **Duck**, quacking away,
Swimming in ponds on a sunny day.

D is for **Door**, that opens wide,
Step on through to the world outside.

D is for **Drum**, with a loud boom-boom,
Making music to fill the room.

D is for **Dinosaur**, big and tall,
Roaring loudly, the king of them all!

D is for **Day**, so bright and new,
With so much to learn and fun things to do!

E is Exciting!

E is for **Elephant**, big and gray,
Swinging its trunk as it walks all day.

E is for **Egg**, round and white,
Crack it open—what a delight!

E is for **Eagle**, soaring so high,
Spreading its wings to glide in the sky.

E is for **Engine**, chugging along,
Pulling the train with a choo-choo song.

E is for **Earth**, where we all stay,
Full of wonders every day!

E is exciting, so many things to see,
Come and explore the letter E with **me**!

F is Fantastic!

F is for **Fish**, swimming so free,
Gliding through rivers and under the sea.

F is for **Frog**, hopping around,
Jumping and croaking with a funny sound.

F is for **Flower**, pretty and bright,
Blooming in colors, a beautiful sight.

F is for **Firetruck**, racing so fast,
Helping put fires out really fast!

F is for **Feather**, soft and light,
Floating gently, such a delight.

F is fantastic, so much fun to say,
Let's learn more about F today!

G is Great!

G is for **Goat**, climbing up high,
Balancing on mountains, reaching the sky.

G is for **Giraffe**, with a neck so long,
Reaching for leaves, where it belongs.

G is for **Garden**, where flowers grow,
With veggies and plants all in a row.

G is for **Gift**, wrapped up so neat,
A surprise inside, oh, what a treat!

G is for **Goldfish**, swimming with glee,
In its tiny bowl, as happy as can be.

G is great, let's give it a cheer,
It's a letter we love, so bright and clear!

H is Happy!

H is for **Horse**, galloping fast,
Racing through fields, it's such a blast!

H is for **House**, cozy and warm,
A place to stay safe from any storm.

H is for **Hat**, sitting on your head,
Keeping you stylish in colors like red.

H is for **Hen**, laying eggs all day,
Clucking around in her special way.

H is for **Heart**, so full of love,
Beating with kindness, like wings of a dove.

H is happy, let's sing it loud,
H is a letter that makes us proud!

I is Incredible!

I is for **Ice cream**, tasty and sweet,
A cool little treat that's fun to eat!

I is for **Igloo**, made out of snow,
A cozy little house where the cold winds blow.

I is for **Inchworm**, crawling so slow,
Measuring the ground wherever it goes.

I is for **Island**, surrounded by sea,
A magical place for you and me!

I is for **Ice**, so frosty and cold,
Perfect for drinks or stories told.

I is incredible, don't you agree?
It's a letter that's fun for you and me!

J is Jolly!

J is for **Jump**, hop high in the air,
Leaping and bouncing without a care!

J is for **Jelly**, so wobbly and sweet,
A jiggly snack that's fun to eat.

J is for **Jaguar**, swift and strong,
Running through jungles all day long.

J is for **Juice**, so tasty and bright,
Orange, apple, or berry—such a delight!

J is for **Jack-in-the-box**, a surprise to see,
Pop goes the toy with a laugh of glee!

J is jolly, let's clap and cheer,
It's a joyful letter we hold so dear!

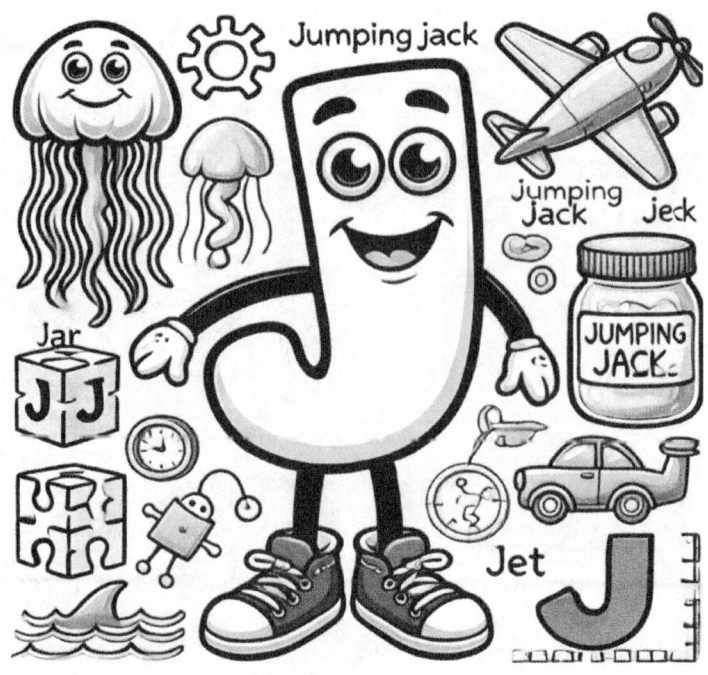

K is Kind and Keen!

K is for **Kite**, flying so high,
Dancing with clouds up in the sky.

K is for **Kangaroo**, hopping around,
With a baby in its pouch, safe and sound.

K is for **King**, with a crown so grand,
Ruling the kingdom, giving commands.

K is for **Key**, to open the door,
Unlocking adventures and treasures galore.

K is for **Koala**, in a tree so tall,
Cuddly and cute, hanging on for it all.

K is kind, it's a letter we know,
Let's learn about K as we watch it grow!

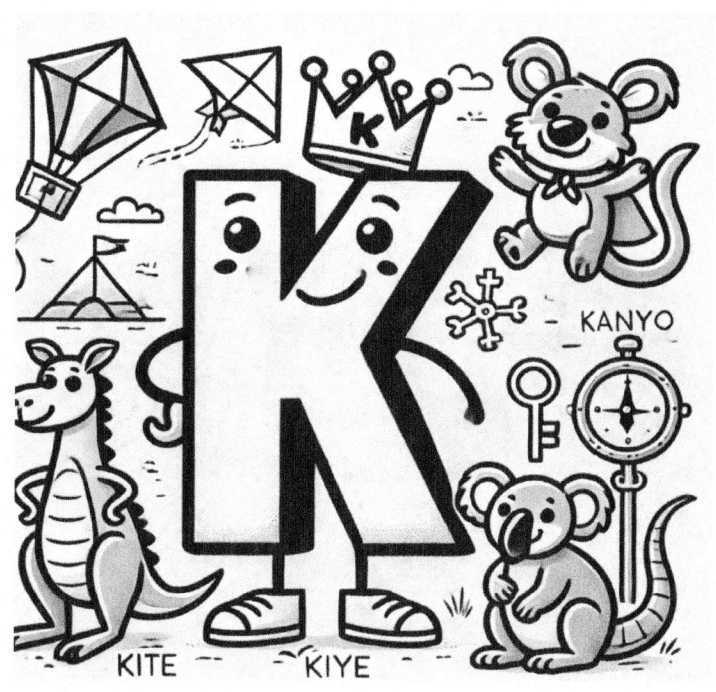

L is Lovely!

L is for **Lion**, so brave and strong,
Roaring loudly all day long.

L is for **Leaf**, green and bright,
Swaying gently in the sunlight.

L is for **Ladder**, climbing so high,
Reaching the stars up in the sky.

L is for **Lollipop**, tasty and sweet,
A colorful treat that's fun to eat.

L is for **Lamp**, that lights up the night,
Keeping us cozy with its warm light.

L is lovely, don't you agree?
It's a letter as fun as can be!

M is Magical!

M is for **Moon**, glowing so bright,
Shining above in the peaceful night.

M is for **Monkey**, swinging in trees,
Chattering happily in the breeze.

M is for **Milk**, creamy and white,
A drink that's healthy, morning or night.

M is for **Mountain**, tall and grand,
Reaching the clouds, touching the land.

M is for **Mittens**, cozy and warm,
Keeping hands safe in the winter storm.

M is magical, full of surprise,
Let's learn about M with wide-open eyes!

N is Nice!

N is for **Nest**, where birds love to stay,
Keeping their eggs safe every day.

N is for **Nut**, crunchy and small,
A tasty snack for squirrels and all.

N is for **Night**, so quiet and dark,
Stars in the sky like a shiny spark.

N is for **Nose**, that helps us smell,
Flowers and cookies we love so well.

N is for **Net**, to catch a fish,
Or play some games, if that's your wish.

N is nice, so neat and new,
Learning about N is fun to do!

O is Outstanding!

O is for **Octopus**, swimming in the sea,
With eight long arms, as busy as can be.

O is for **Orange**, juicy and round,
A fruit that's delicious and easily found.

O is for **Owl**, awake at night,
Hooting softly in the pale moonlight.

O is for **Ocean**, wide and deep,
With waves that crash and fish that leap.

O is for **Oval**, a fun shape to find,
Like eggs or balloons, it's one of a kind.

O is outstanding, let's cheer and say,
Learning about O brightens our day!

P is Perfect!

P is for **Penguin**, waddling away,
Sliding on ice, so happy to play.

P is for **Pineapple**, spiky and sweet,
A tropical treat that's fun to eat.

P is for **Parrot**, colorful and bright,
Chattering words with all its might.

P is for **Pencil**, to draw and write,
Creating pictures, day or night.

P is for **Plane**, soaring so high,
Flying above the clouds in the sky.

P is perfect, so full of fun,
Let's learn about P, it's loved by everyone!

Q is Quite Quirky!

Q is for **Queen**, with a crown so grand,
Ruling the kingdom with a wave of her hand.

Q is for **Quilt**, so cozy and warm,
Keeping you snug through the coldest storm.

Q is for **Quail**, a bird so small,
Running and hopping, not flying at all.

Q is for **Quarter**, shiny and round,
A coin to treasure when it's found.

Q is for **Quiet**, a time to rest,
Close your eyes, and feel your best.

Q is quite quirky, it's a letter to see,
Let's all shout, "Hooray for Q and me!"

R is Remarkable!

R is for **Rabbit**, so quick and so cute,
Hopping around in a fluffy suit.

R is for **Rainbow**, with colors so bright,
Shining after rain, a magical sight.

R is for **Rocket**, blasting to space,
Zooming past stars in a thrilling race.

R is for **Rose**, so lovely and red,
A flower that blooms in the garden bed.

R is for **River**, flowing so free,
Carrying water to the deep blue sea.

R is remarkable, it's fun to explore,
Let's learn about R and so much more!

S is Super!

S is for **Sun**, shining so bright,
Lighting the world with its golden light.

S is for **Snake**, slithering around,
Hissing softly without a sound.

S is for **Star**, sparkling at night,
Twinkling above, a magical sight.

S is for **Strawberry**, juicy and red,
A sweet little treat for tummy and head.

S is for **Snow**, so soft and white,
Falling from clouds, a winter delight.

S is super, so special to see,
Let's learn about S, just you and me!

T is Terrific!

T is for **Tiger**, strong and bold,
With orange stripes and a heart of gold.

T is for **Train**, chugging along,
Clickety-clack with a whistle song.

T is for **Tree**, so tall and green,
Home to birds and a peaceful scene.

T is for **Turtle**, slow but sweet,
Walking carefully on tiny feet.

T is for **Truck**, big and loud,
Driving by, it makes us proud!

T is terrific, full of delight,
Let's learn about T, morning and night!

U is Unique!

U is for **Umbrella**, keeping you dry,
Under the rain or the cloudy sky.

U is for **Unicorn**, magical and bright,
A creature of dreams, a wonderful sight.

U is for **Utensils**, a fork and a spoon,
Helping us eat lunch, dinner, and noon.

U is for **Up**, where balloons like to go,
Floating high above, putting on a show.

U is for **Under**, a place you can hide,
Maybe under a table or a blanket inside.

U is unique, it's special and true,
Let's learn about U, me and you!

V is Vibrant!

V is for **Violin**, making sweet sound,
Music so lovely, it dances around.

V is for **Vase**, holding flowers so bright,
A splash of color, such a delight.

V is for **Van**, driving near and far,
Carrying people, just like a car.

V is for **Vegetables**, healthy and green,
Carrots and broccoli, a crunchy cuisine.

V is vibrant, it's fun to say,
Let's learn about V in every way!

W is Wonderful!

W is for **Whale**, so big and so strong,
Swimming in the ocean all day long.

W is for **Wind**, blowing the trees,
Whistling softly in the gentle breeze.

W is for **Watermelon**, juicy and sweet,
A summertime snack, a cool little treat.

W is for **Wagon**, to pull your toys,
Carrying treasures for girls and boys.

W is wonderful, let's give it a cheer,
Learning about W is fun and clear!

X is Exciting!

X is for **Xylophone**, playing a tune,
Tapping the keys under the moon.

X is for **X-ray**, showing what's inside,
Looking at bones that like to hide.

X is for words with a hidden **X**,
Like fox and box, what's coming next?

X is exciting, a letter to see,
Let's find more words with X, just you and me!

Y is Yummy!

Y is for **Yogurt**, creamy and smooth,
A tasty snack that puts you in the mood.

Y is for **Yo-yo**, spinning so fast,
Up and down, what a blast!

Y is for **Yellow**, the color of sun,
Bright and cheerful, it's so much fun.

Y is for **Yak**, with long, shaggy hair,
Living in the mountains, without a care.

Y is yummy, it's special and bright,
Let's learn about Y with all our might!

Z is Zany!

Z is for **Zebra**, with stripes so neat,
Running through grasslands on fast little feet.

Z is for **Zoo**, with animals to see,
Lions, and tigers, and monkeys in trees.

Z is for **Zipper**, going up and down,
Keeping your coat snug all around.

Z is for **Zucchini**, a veggie that's great,
Cook it for dinner and put it on your plate.

Z is zany, the last letter to know,
Let's give it a shout before we go!

PART II

The Numbers
Practice counting numbers (1-10 and progressing to 1-20).

Counting Fun from 1 to 10

1 is the **sun**, shining so bright,
Waking the world with its golden light.

2 are my **shoes**, a pair on my feet,
Walking together, so tidy and neat.

3 are the **trees**, so tall and so green,
Waving their branches in the breeze unseen.

4 are the **doors**, that open so wide,
Letting us through to the world outside.

5 are the **bees**, buzzing with glee,
Flying to flowers as busy as can be.

6 are the **sticks**, laid out in a row,
Pick them up and off we go!

7 are the **stars**, twinkling at night,
Sparkling softly with silvery light.

8 is the **spider**, with legs long and thin,
Spinning a web to catch what comes in.

9 are the **balloons**, floating up high,
Colors like rainbows filling the sky.

10 are my **fingers**, wiggle and bend,
Counting them all—let's do it again!

1 to 10, now you can say,
Numbers are fun to learn and play!

Number One

Number **1**, so straight and tall,
The first to count, it starts them all!
Like the bright sun up in the sky,
Shining alone, so bold and high!

Number Two

Number 2 is fun to see,
A duck in water or birds in a tree.
Two little hands, a perfect pair,
Clapping together here and there!

Number Three

Number **3** is easy to see,
Like bumpy hills or waves at sea.
Three little kittens playing in a row,
Laughing and jumping wherever they go!

Number Four

Number **4** is neat and square,
Four legs on a chair to hold you there.
Four little wheels to make a car go,
Rolling along, steady and slow!

Number Five

Number **5** is full of fun,
Five fingers waving, one by one.
Five little ducks in a pond so blue,
Quacking and splashing, just for you!

Number Six

Number **6** is a curvy delight,
Like a snail shell, tucked in tight.
Six buzzing bees fly flower to flower,
Gathering nectar hour by hour!

Number Seven

Number 7, a lucky line,
Shaped like a step, it's simply divine.
Seven bright stars in the evening sky,
Twinkling softly as night drifts by!

Number Eight

Number **8** is a loop so round,
Two circles stacked, a shape profound.
Like a snowman standing tall and straight,
Eight is a number that's truly great!

Number Nine

Number **9** is a loop with a line,
Standing tall, it looks so fine.
Nine balloons float up so high,
Dancing brightly in the sky!

Number Zero

Number 0, a perfect ring,
Round and empty, a curious thing.
It starts our count, yet stands alone,
A circle of magic, all its own!

Number Ten

Number **10** stands proud and tall,
A **1** and **0**, the start of it all.
It leads the way, the counting's begun,
The journey starts with **10** and **1**!

PART III

Recognizing Shapes
Identify basic shapes like circles, squares, and triangles.

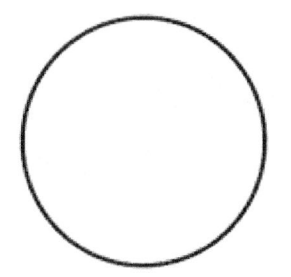

Circle

A round shape with no corners.
It looks like a wheel, a coin, or the sun.

Square

A shape with four equal sides and four corners.
It looks like a box or a window.

Triangle

A shape with three sides and three corners.
It looks like a slice of pizza or a mountain.

Rectangle

A shape with four sides and four corners.
It looks like a door or a book.

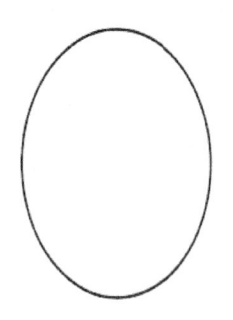

Oval

A stretched-out circle.
It looks like an egg or a balloon.

Star

A shape with five or more points.
It looks like the twinkling stars in the night sky.

Heart

A shape that looks like love.
It's round at the top and pointy at the bottom.

Diamond

A shape with four sides, like a square turned on its corner.
It looks like a kite.

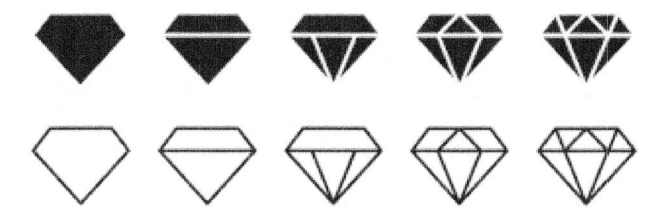

Pentagon

A shape with five sides.
It looks like a house with a flat roof.

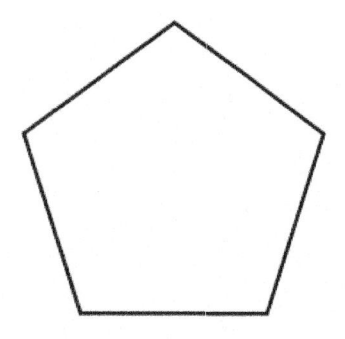

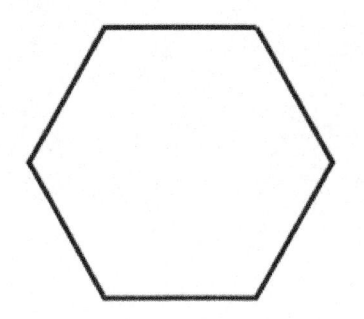

Hexagon

A shape with six sides.
It looks like a honeycomb from a beehive.

PART IV

Understanding sizes
Understanding sizes (big/small, long/short)

Decide which object is bigger and which is smaller.

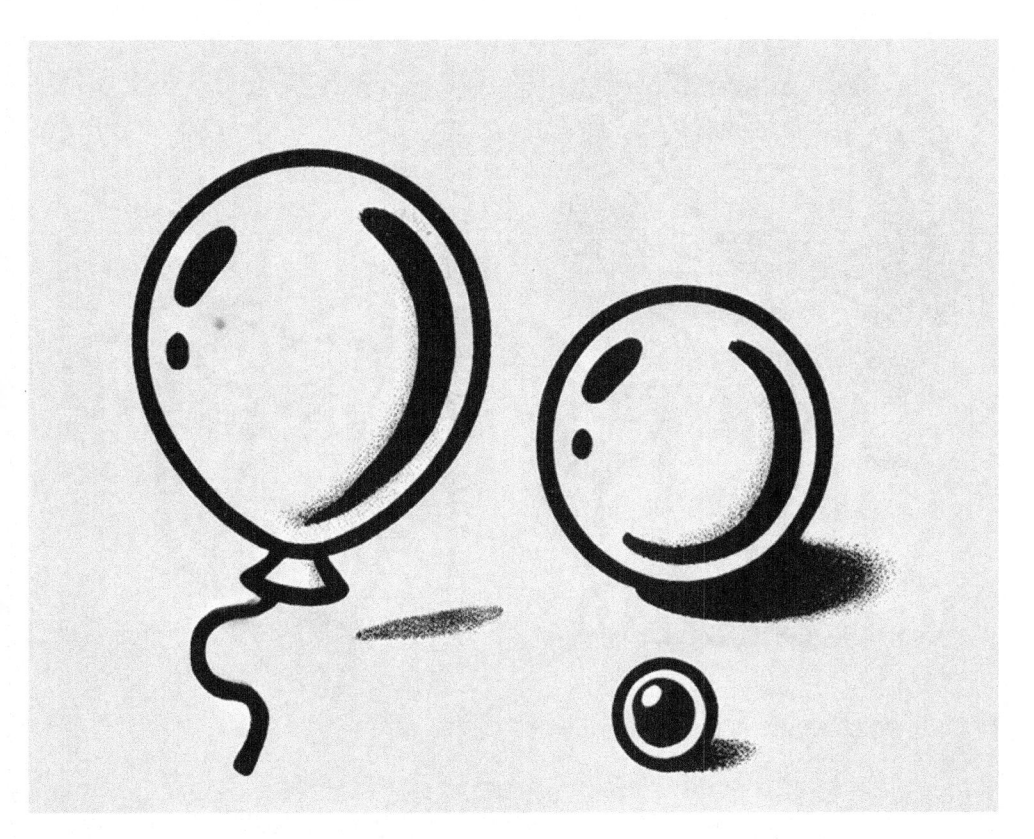

Decide which bike is bigger and which is smaller.

Decide which animal is bigger and which is smaller.

Decide which apple is bigger and which is smaller.

Decide which fruit is bigger and which is smaller.

Find the longer object:

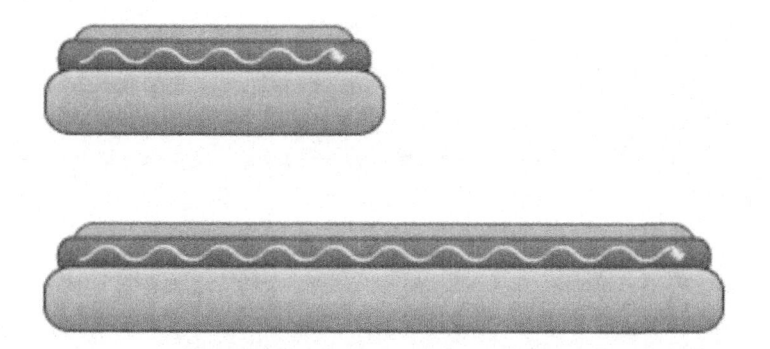

Decide which fruit is bigger and which is smaller.

Find the longer object:

Decide which fruit is bigger and which is smaller.

Find the shorter object:

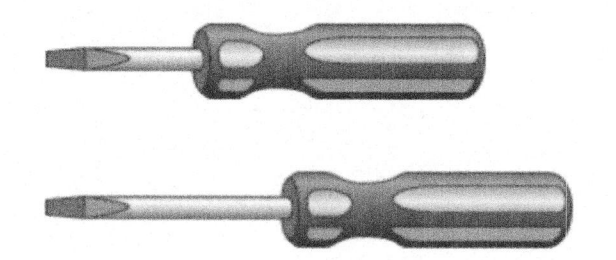

53 | P a g e

Circle the one that is bigger:

- A watermelon or an apple
- An elephant or a dog
- A car or a bicycle
- The moon or a star in the sky
- A tree or a flower
- A mountain or a hill
- A house or a tent
- A lion or a mouse
- A balloon or a marble
- The ocean or a swimming pool

Find the longer object:

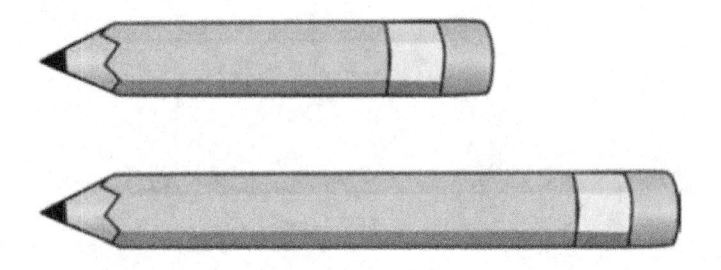

Find the shorter object:

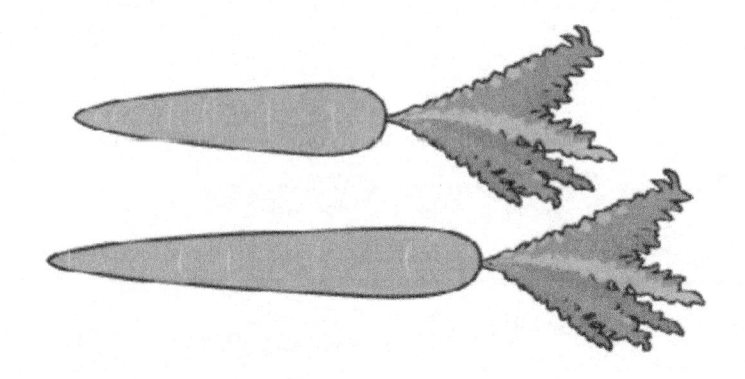

PART V

Seasons and Weather
Exploring seasons and weather (sun, rain, snow)

Guess, what weather is outside?

SUN
RAIN
SNOW

How do think which picture has the warmest weather / the coldest?

How many pictures have clouds?

What weather condition you see here, mark all:

Sun	Cloud	Snow
Rain	Wind	Cold
Hot	Mountain	Ocean
Forest	Beach	Cave

What weather condition you see here, mark all:

Sun	Cloud	Snow
Rain	Wind	Cold
Hot	House	Ocean
Forest	Beach	Puddle

What weather condition you see here, mark all:

Sun	Cloud	Snow
Rain	Wind	Cold
Hot	House	Ocean
Forest	Beach	Snowflake

Recognize seasons:

What season is it? _____

What season is it? _____

What season is it? _____

What season is it? _____

PART VI

Hygiene
Understanding basic hygiene

Wash Your Hands

Always wash your hands, it's easy to do,
With soap and water, a healthy rule for you!
Before you eat or touch your face,
Wash those germs right out of place.

After the bathroom or playing outside,
Keep your hands clean with water as your guide.
Scrub them gently, let the bubbles grow,
Rinse them off and watch them glow!

Clean hands help you stay strong each day,
So wash them often, it's the safest way!

Brush Your Teeth Twice a Day

Brush your teeth, it's easy to do,
In the morning and night, just for you.
Keep them clean, shiny, and bright,
Healthy teeth make your smile just right!

Grab your brush and toothpaste too,
Scrub each tooth, the top and the crew.
Don't forget your gums and tongue,
Fresh and clean when the day is begun!

At bedtime, it's the final chore,
Brush again to fight germs galore.
Twice a day, it's the healthy way,
Keep your teeth strong every day!

Cover Your Mouth and Nose:

When you sneeze or cough, use your elbow or a tissue to keep germs from spreading.

Stay Clean and Fresh

Take a bath, splash here and there,
Wash your body with love and care.
Soap and water, scrub-a-dub-dub,
Rinse off dirt in the bubbly tub!

Put on clothes, so fresh and neat,
Clean and tidy, head to feet.
Comb your hair, make it shine,
You'll look and feel so very fine!

Stay clean and fresh, it's easy to do,
A healthy habit just for you!

PART VII

Body Parts
Learn Body Parts and Their Functions

Know Your Body

Your **head** holds your brain, where thinking is done,
It helps you imagine and learn while you have fun!
Your **eyes** help you see the world so wide,
Colors and shapes, all seen with pride.

Your **ears** hear music, laughter, and sound,
They catch every noise, all around!
Your **arms** and **hands** hold, hug, and play,
They carry your toys and wave "Hooray!"

Your **legs** and **feet** help you jump and run,
Taking you places, under the sun.
Each body part has a job to do,
Learning about them is fun for you!

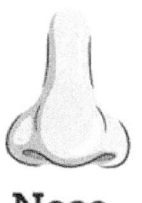

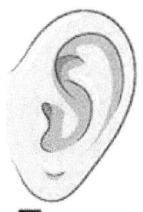

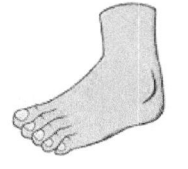

Nose	Ears	Eyes	Feet	Sole
Tongue	Lips	Teeth	Mustache	

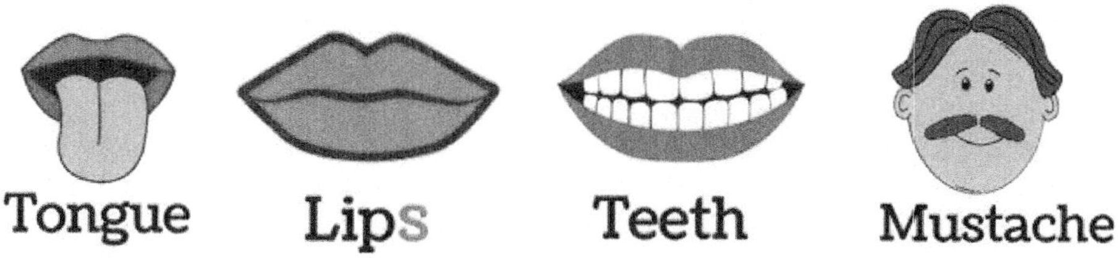

Our five sense organs each play a different role in our ability to perform various tasks:

- Sight,
- Hearing,
- Smell,
- Tongue,
- Skin

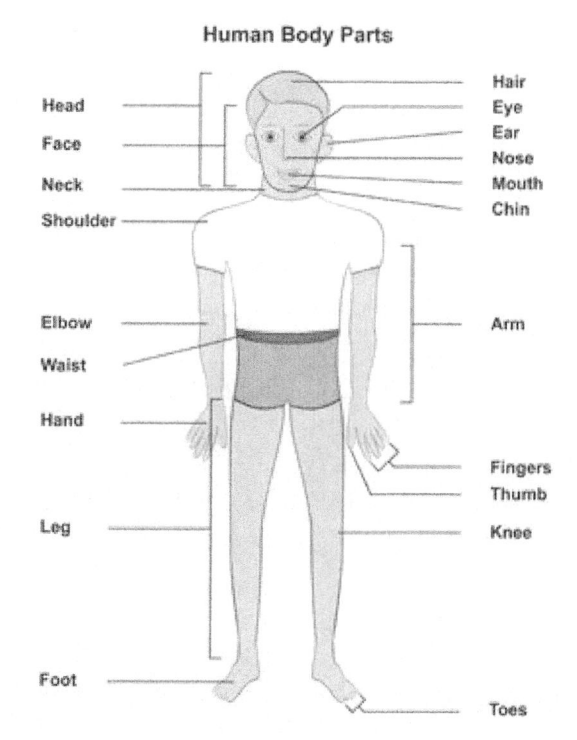

Human Body Parts

Labels: Head, Face, Neck, Shoulder, Elbow, Waist, Hand, Leg, Foot, Hair, Eye, Ear, Nose, Mouth, Chin, Arm, Fingers, Thumb, Knee, Toes

External Body Parts

- **Head**: The head is at the top of your body. It holds your brain and important parts like your eyes, ears, nose, and mouth.

- **Skin**: Your skin covers your whole body. It keeps you safe by blocking germs and dirt.

- **Limbs**: Your arms and legs are called limbs. They help you move, play, and hold things.

- **Eyes**: Your eyes help you see the world around you—colors, shapes, and everything fun!

- **Ears**: Your ears help you hear sounds, like music, voices, and even animals! They also help you keep your balance.

- **Nose**: Your nose helps you smell flowers, food, and many other things. It also helps you breathe.

- **Mouth**: Your mouth helps you eat, talk, and taste yummy food.

- **Neck**: Your neck connects your head to your body and helps you turn your head.

- **Shoulders**: Your shoulders connect your arms to your body. They let you lift and carry things.

- **Chest**: Your chest holds important parts like your heart and lungs. It's the part of your body between your neck and belly.

- **Hips**: Your hips are the bones on the sides of your body, near your upper legs. They help you sit, stand, and move.

- **Buttocks**: Your buttocks are muscles at the back of your body. They help you sit comfortably.

Internal Body Parts

- **Heart**: Your heart is like a pump. It moves blood all around your body to keep you alive.

- **Lungs**: Your lungs help you breathe. They take in oxygen and send it to your blood while getting rid of carbon dioxide.

- **Liver**: Your liver helps your body clean itself and turn food into energy.

- **Kidneys**: Your kidneys clean your blood and make urine, which helps remove waste.

- **Stomach**: Your stomach is where food goes after you eat. It helps break the food down for energy.

- **Brain**: Your brain is like the boss of your body. It helps you think, feel, and control everything you do.

- **Intestines**: Your intestines are tubes that help your body take in nutrients from food and get rid of what's left.

- **Pancreas**: Your pancreas helps your body control sugar levels and digest food.

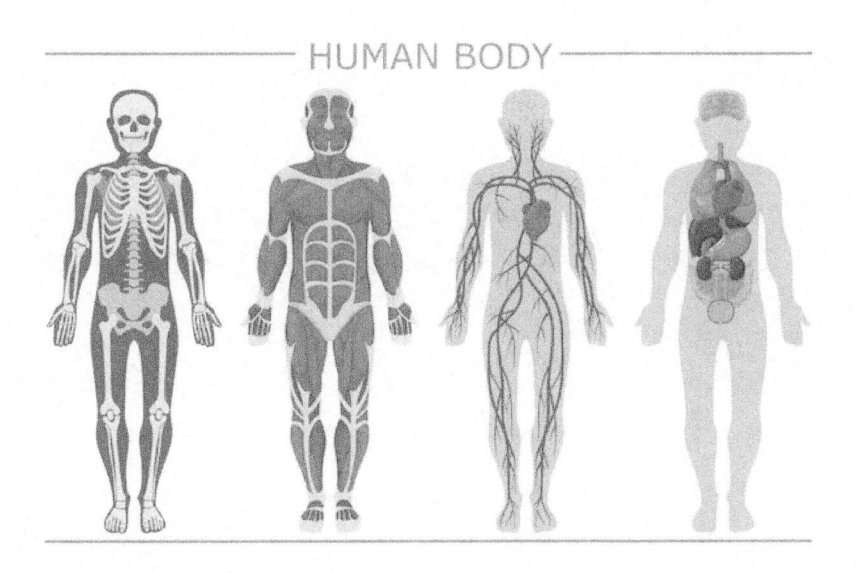

PART VIII

Family & Relationship
Recognizing family roles and relationships

Recognizing Family Roles and Relationships

Families are special groups of people who love and care for each other. Everyone in a family has an important role to play. Understanding these roles helps us appreciate our family members and how we work together as a team.

What Is a Family?

A family is a group of people who care about each other. Families can be big or small. Some families live together in the same house, while others may live in different places but still love each other very much. A family can include parents, grandparents, brothers, sisters, aunts, uncles, cousins, and more. Every family is unique, and that's what makes them special!

Who Are the People in a Family?

1. Parents
Parents are the grown-ups who take care of you. They might be your mom, dad, or both. Parents love you, help you learn, and make sure you have everything you need. They might cook yummy meals, help with homework, or tuck you into bed at night. Moms and dads also teach us how to be kind, honest, and responsible.
- **Fun Role:** Parents are like superheroes! They work hard to keep the family happy and safe.

2. Siblings
Siblings are your brothers and sisters. If you have a sibling, you can play, share, and learn from each other. Sometimes you might argue, but that's okay because you love each other and always make up.
- **Fun Role:** Siblings are like built-in friends. They help you learn teamwork and sharing.

3. Grandparents
Grandparents are your mom's or dad's parents. They are wise and full of stories about when they were young. Grandparents love to spoil their grandchildren with hugs, treats, and fun surprises.
- **Fun Role:** Grandparents are like storytellers and treasure keepers of the family's past.

4. Aunts and Uncles
Aunts and uncles are your parents' brothers and sisters. They are fun and loving and sometimes act like extra parents. They might take you on adventures or teach you something new.
- **Fun Role:** Aunts and uncles are like cool coaches who cheer you on.

5. Cousins
Cousins are the children of your aunts and uncles. They can be your age, younger, or older. Cousins are like extra brothers and sisters. You can play games, have fun, and make great memories together.
- **Fun Role:** Cousins are like teammates who share family adventures.

What Are Family Roles?

Every family member has a role or job that helps the family work as a team. Let's look at some of the important roles:

1. The Caretaker

This is someone who makes sure everyone is safe and happy. Parents are usually the main caretakers, but sometimes older siblings or grandparents can help too.

- **Example:** Mom makes sure you eat healthy meals, and Dad reminds you to wear your coat when it's cold.

2. The Helper
Helpers lend a hand with chores or tasks. Kids can be helpers too! Maybe you set the table for dinner, or your big sister helps you tie your shoes.
- **Example:** Cleaning up toys together is a great way to be a helper.

3. The Listener
A listener is someone who pays attention when another family member talks. Grandparents are great listeners because they love hearing about your day.
- **Example:** When you tell your mom about school, she listens carefully and gives you advice.

4. The Teacher

Teachers help others learn new things. Parents teach you how to read, and siblings might show you how to ride a bike.
- **Example:** Your dad teaches you how to bake cookies, or your grandma shows you how to knit.

5. The Cheerleader

Cheerleaders support and encourage you when you try something new. They clap when you do a great job and tell you to keep going when it's hard.
- **Example:** Your aunt cheers for you at your soccer game, or your brother says, "You can do it!" when you're learning to swim.

Why Are Family Roles Important?

Family roles help everyone feel special and loved. They also teach us teamwork. When everyone works together, the family is happy and strong. Knowing what each person does helps us understand how to help each other and show kindness.

How Can You Help in Your Family?

Even kids have important roles in the family! Here are some ways you can help:

- **Be a Helper:** Clean up your toys, feed the family pet, or water the plants.
- **Be a Listener:** Pay attention when your parents, siblings, or grandparents talk to you.
- **Be Kind:** Say thank you, give hugs, and share with your siblings.
- **Be Responsible:** Do your homework, brush your teeth, and keep your room tidy.
- **Be a Cheerleader:** Encourage your siblings when they try something new, like learning to ride a bike.

Fun Activities to Learn About Family Roles

Here are some activities to help you understand and enjoy your family relationships:

- **Family Tree:** Draw a tree and add the names of your family members. You can even include pictures or drawings of them.
- **Role Play:** Pretend to be different family members for a day. For example, act like Mom or Dad and see how it feels to take care of others.
- **Thank You Notes:** Write or draw thank-you notes for your family members to show you appreciate what they do.
- **Chore Chart:** Create a chart with small tasks for everyone in the family. Check off the tasks as they get done.
- **Story Time:** Ask your grandparents to tell you stories about when they were kids. You'll learn so much about your family's history!

Family Love and Respect

Every family is built on love and respect. Here's how you can show love and respect to your family:

- **Say Kind Words:** Use words like "please," "thank you," and "I love you."
- **Share:** Share your toys, snacks, or even hugs.
- **Help Each Other:** Offer help when someone needs it, like carrying groceries or setting the table.
- **Be Honest:** Always tell the truth and keep promises.
- **Apologize:** If you make a mistake, say sorry and try to make it right.

Family Love

A family is a team, so loving and true,
With special roles for me and for you.
Parents who guide, siblings who share,
Grandparents who show us how much they care.

Together we laugh, we learn, and we play,
Helping each other every day.
A family's love is big and strong,
Where everyone feels they belong!

Remember: Every family is special in its own way. Learning about family roles and relationships helps you feel connected and loved. Your family is your team, and you are an important part of it! So, always cherish your family and show them how much you care.

PART IX

Maze
Completing simple mazes \
Identifying differences and similarities

Find the road to the moon:

Find 10 differences:

Help cook to find dishes:

Identify 10 differences:

Identify 10 differences:

Find the exit:

Find 10 differences:

Find the exit:

PART X

Good Manners
Practicing good manners (please, thank you)

Practicing Good Manners: Please and Thank You

Good manners are like magic words that make everyone feel happy and respected. When you say "please" and "thank you," you show kindness and make the people around you smile. Learning and practicing good manners is very important, and it's also fun! Let's explore how saying these simple words can make a big difference.

What Are Good Manners?

Good manners are ways we show respect and kindness to others. They are like little rules that help us get along with family, friends, teachers, and even people we don't know very well. When you use good manners, you make the world a better place by being polite and thoughtful.

Why Are Please and Thank You Important?

The words "please" and "thank you" are very powerful. They show that you care about other people and appreciate what they do for you. Let's break it down:
- Please: This word is like a magic key that opens doors. When you say "please," you ask for something in a kind and respectful way.
- Thank You: This is how you show appreciation when someone helps you or gives you something. It's a way to say, "I'm grateful."

Using these words makes people feel happy and helps them see that you have good manners.

How to Use "Please"

Here are some examples of when you can use "please":
- When Asking for Help: "Can you please help me tie my shoes?"
- When Requesting Something: "May I please have a cookie?"
- When Playing: "Can I please have a turn on the swing?"

Saying "please" makes your request polite and shows that you respect the other person.

How to Use "Thank You"

Here are some examples of when you can use "thank you":
- When Receiving Something: "Thank you for the gift!"
- When Someone Helps You: "Thank you for holding the door for me."
- When Someone Gives You a Compliment: "Thank you! That's so nice of you to say."

Saying "thank you" shows that you appreciate what others do for you.

Good Manners at Home

Practicing good manners starts at home. Here are some ways you can use "please" and "thank you" with your family:
1. Asking for Food: When you want seconds at dinner, say, "May I please have more pasta?"
2. Helping Around the House: When someone helps you with a chore, say, "Thank you for helping me clean my room!"
3. Sharing with Siblings: When you want to borrow a toy, say, "Can I please play with your truck?"

When everyone in the family uses good manners, the home feels happier and more peaceful.

Good Manners at School

Using "please" and "thank you" at school shows respect for your teachers and classmates. Here's how you can practice good manners at school:
1. Asking for Help in Class: If you need help with your work, say, "Can you please help me with this math problem?"
2. Thanking Your Teacher: When your teacher gives you advice or helps you learn, say, "Thank you for explaining that to me."
3. Sharing with Friends: If a friend lets you borrow a crayon, say, "Thank you for sharing with me!"

Good manners help you make friends and show your teacher that you are respectful.

Good Manners in Public

When you are in public places, like a park or a store, good manners are very important. Here are some examples:
1. At the Park: If you want to use the slide, say, "Can I please have a turn?"
2. At a Store: When someone helps you find what you're looking for, say, "Thank you for your help."
3. On the Bus: If someone lets you sit down, say, "Thank you for the seat."

Using good manners in public makes you a polite and kind person.

How Good Manners Make People Feel

When you use good manners, you make others feel happy and respected. Imagine this:
- If you say "please" when you ask for a cookie, the person giving it to you feels appreciated.
- If you say "thank you" when someone helps you pick up your toys, they feel proud and happy to help.

Good manners spread kindness and make the world a better place.

Good Manners

Good manners are simple, as easy as can be,
A way to show kindness to you and to me.
Say "please" when you ask, it's polite to do,
And remember to say "thank you" too!

At home, at school, or when you're out,
Good manners are what kindness is about.
So practice them daily, in all that you say,
Being polite makes a brighter day!

PART XI

Friendship
Understanding friendships and cooperation

Understanding Friendships and Cooperation

Friendships are one of the most special parts of life. Friends make us laugh, help us when we're feeling sad, and share fun moments with us. But being a good friend means more than just having fun—it means learning how to work together, share, and care for each other. Let's explore what friendships and cooperation mean and how we can build strong relationships with the people around us.

What Is Friendship?

Friendship is when two or more people like spending time together and care about each other. Friends are people who make us happy, play with us, and support us when we need help. Friends can be classmates, neighbors, or even family members. What makes a friendship strong is kindness, trust, and teamwork.

Here are a few ways to know someone is your friend:
1. They make you feel happy and included.
2. They share and take turns.
3. They listen when you talk.
4. They care about your feelings.

Why Are Friends Important?

Friends make life fun and exciting! They help us:

- **Have Fun:** Friends make games, school, and playtime better.
- **Learn New Things:** Friends can teach us how to play new games or solve puzzles.
- **Feel Supported:** When we are sad or scared, friends cheer us up.
- **Grow Together:** Friends help us learn how to be kind, share, and solve problems.

Having good friends helps us feel happy and strong inside.

What Is Cooperation?

Cooperation means working together to reach a goal. It's like being on a team where everyone helps each other. Cooperation is important at home, school, and when playing games. When we cooperate, we learn how to listen, share, and solve problems together.

Here are some examples of cooperation:
- Helping your friend build a tower of blocks.
- Cleaning up toys together after playtime.
- Working with your classmates on a group project.

How to Be a Good Friend

Being a good friend means treating others the way you want to be treated. Here are some tips for being a great friend:

1. Share and Take Turns

Friends share toys, snacks, and time. If you're playing a game, take turns so everyone gets to play. Sharing shows that you care about your friends' happiness.

- Example: If you have a toy car, let your friend have a turn driving it.

2. Be Kind
Kind words and actions make friends feel special. Say things like, "You did a great job!" or "I'm so glad we're friends."
- Example: If your friend falls, help them up and say, "Are you okay?"

3. Listen and Care
When your friend talks, listen carefully. Show that you care about what they're saying by looking at them and nodding.
- Example: If your friend tells you about their new pet, listen and ask questions like, "What's its name?"

4. Say Sorry When You Need To

Sometimes, we make mistakes, and that's okay! Saying "sorry" helps fix hurt feelings and shows your friend that you care.

- Example: If you accidentally knock over your friend's blocks, say, "I'm sorry. Let me help you rebuild it."

Cooperation makes playing and working together easier and more fun.

Friendship and Cooperation

Friends are like sunshine, bright and warm,
They're there to cheer us through every storm.
Sharing, caring, and working as a team,
Together we're stronger—a wonderful dream!

Cooperation helps us grow each day,
Learning, playing, the kindest way.
With friends by our side, we'll always do,
Great things together, me and you!

Why Friendships and Cooperation Matter

Friendships and cooperation teach us how to:
- Be kind and respectful.
- Share and take turns.
- Solve problems and work as a team.
- Build trust and strong relationships.

When we practice being good friends and working together, we make our world a happier and better place.

Printed in Great Britain
by Amazon